THE JOURNEY OF
PEACE AND PURPOSE

JEREMY WRIGHT

Dedicated to:

Future generations

Book Intention and the Journey of Peace and Purpose

The intention of this book is to help lay a solid foundation for my future generations by revisiting where I was at different points in my journey of peace and purpose. My hope is that future generations will allow my lessons learned and reflections to be a compass that navigates them throughout life in a way that helps them to quickly find inner peace and their purpose in life. This labor of love comes from a place of giving what I wish was given to me at an early age. I simply aim to guide and not direct, as my life is already in the process of being lived. One of many precious gifts any loved one can give to another is that of a clear path to peace and purpose.

Dear Me,

Breathe. Center yourself in the present moment. Be grateful. Keep moving with positive intention. Despite the many odds that were against us, over the past few years we have been doing the work that has readied us for what lies ahead. Work that will require consistent and conscious choices aligned with purpose. Work that may require more late nights, early mornings, flying into different time zones, going into unchartered territories, challenging the status quo, and so much more. Nothing can stop us if we maintain positive intentions, operate from a place of peace, and make decisions in alignment with honoring our purpose.

Not only have we laid a path for others to obtain peace and purpose, but we have contributed to a movement of individuals who are reaching to the core of who they are to live a more authentic life. Pouring our purpose in the form of books, coaching, and speaking has allowed us to water the seeds that have been planted along the way, making it easier for others to make it through this difficult journey. To consider the weight of generational trauma that we carried on our shoulders and where we are now is incomprehensible and a miracle. Job well done for shifting life in favor of those who come behind us. Although this may seem like the end of the journey, it is only just begun.

With all the unconditional love from within,

The ME behind me

Dear Reader,

I do not know if I will have children of my own, but I do have nieces, nephews, cousins, and godchildren. Even with the thought of not having children, I still feel the responsibility to guide the next generation toward a life of inner peace and purpose, so that they can live the life they deserve. Even if I am not around, I want to leave a mark in life for them and everyone else in their generations of possibility when a life of peace and purpose is the goal. To them, in their youth, these things may not make sense, but as life unfolds, things will be revealed. I hope that these books find them and act like guiding stars in dark nights, leading them to a life that I imagine for them; nothing but the best.

I hope that you walk away realizing the impact that you have on everyone around you based on the decisions that you make. Whether family, people from the same background, or different backgrounds, what do you lose from trying to make life better for the next generation? What do you gain by leaving the next generation to figure it out on their own as we have? Clearly, we can see where that has gotten us based on our lives as a collective today. Let us choose to do the work now so that all can live a life of peace and purpose. We should do what we wish someone had done for us, so that we could have and hopefully will live the life that we deserve.

With all of the unconditional love that I have,

Jeremy

From My Mom with Love

Dear Me,

I am so proud of you! I know this was a hard and lonely journey, but it is not over. We have made decisions that we must live with, but in spite of them, we are still standing. We did the best with what we had, and I forgive us knowing that we were trying to stop the madness that we were enduring and trying to find love. Some of our decisions, although with good intent, brought about challenging relationships, truly lessons in disguise.

The most important relationship that I had to develop was the relationship with myself. This required getting to know me in a way that I never thought I would. Knowing how I defined love and desired it to be shown to me, what triggers certain emotions, and simply how to use my voice, was an important part of this journey that I am still in the process of. While on this journey and reflecting over my life, I have taken the hurts and disappointments to find the lesson within them. I had to find the lesson in each circumstance that I missed when we were trying to find peace, joy, and love.

Having started this relationship with ourselves and the wisdom we have gained, it has become easier to keep pressing forward. Knowing that we want peace and joy, we will not be afraid to take advantage of opportunities in life. The difference between now and then is consistently applying the lessons we have learned. Once we have completed this journey of peace and purpose, we will be able to understand our purpose in life and live our fullest potential and I AM LOOKING FORWARD TO IT!! The sky is, have been, and will always be the limit.

Giving Myself the Best of Me,
Vickie

Dear Reader,

After reading this book, I would like you to be able to let go of the thoughts and emotions that are holding you hostage, the thoughts and emotions that have caused pain that may never be acknowledged by the offender. Know that the offense was not about you, but the brokenness of the person who hurt you. When we are hurting, unknowingly we inflict our pain upon others through our words and/or actions. As you reflect on the offenses that you may have endured, consider how they may have impacted your everyday life.

Take me, for example, I suffered years of sexual abuse. When a friend of mine would tell me that I was who I was because of all the things that had happened to me, all I could think of was the awful things and *that was not me*. It took me a very long time to realize that I was a broken soul. Once I gave myself permission to accept that it happened and not that it was right, I had the space to see how the awful things I thought of, in addition to the good things, made me who I am.

Now that I know why I react the way I do to certain things, people, and places, I am learning to let go of thoughts and emotions, making space for me to be my best self. This is what I hope for you in letting go, to make space for the best version of yourself while on the journey of peace and purpose. You are not *what* has happened to you; you are much more than that. You are an overcomer!

With Much Love,
Vickie

Author Updates

Today is June 8, 2022, and I turned thirty-three. I rented a lake house and my dream car as a nod to a journey of self. I wanted to use this as a means to manifest the life I desired. My mom and I are spending time restoring our capacity so that we can go back into the world refreshed and more aligned with peace and purpose than when we got here. My fourth book, *Well to the Soul: Pouring from a Full Vessel* has just been delivered, and I have just submitted my fifth book for editing. The journey of this book series is coming to an end in its current phase which will allow me the necessary capacity to focus on the next phase.

The more I experience in life, the more I realize how possible it is to dream more. As someone raised as an only child, introverted and creative, I can come up with some very unique things. I have to give it to myself, my next plan will make a mark larger than expected. To trace back everything that I had a liking to, such as music, movies, and more, and understand how it will shape this next phase of the Peace and Purpose series is incomprehensible. What I will share is that the good, the bad, and the ugly of my life make sense more than it ever has. I am in a place of inner peace. I am aligned with my purpose. I recognize my capacity, and I am jumping into every opportunity I have as if generations depend on it.

The Journey of
Peace and Purpose

These letters were written in the previous books of the Peace and Purpose series to capture my personal progress, what I wanted the reader to take away from the respective book, and what I wanted future generations to learn and apply to their lives. Although my thinking and writing have evolved over the years, it is clear that my alignment with the source or God made it possible for me to make the incomprehensible human experience easy to understand. To acknowledge the enormity of the human experience and translate it into writings that the mind can comprehend suggest that I am a vessel being used for a larger purpose. For the sake of ensuring that future generations have a clear path to peace and purpose, let us reflect on my journey of breaking the cycle, trusting the process, releasing to receive, chasing purpose, and abundance.

A Gift of Peace and Purpose: A Survivor's Journey

Dear Me,

After a two-year journey of pressing through to the other side of the lessons that you were meant to learn in order to be where you are, you made it, and it is time to get to work. Although life and learning does not stop here, you now have an understanding of what it is to truly be alive, to be at peace, and to be in total alignment with the reason you are alive. Your "mistakes," the people you encountered, and the circumstances you were in, were all a part of the plan that was laid for you and the decisions you made with free will. This plan was designed to help your soul accomplish things that it needs to accomplish in this lifetime, and as you submit to the process of the plan unfolding, your life blesses you abundantly in ways that you can never fathom. Your process forced you to disconnect from everything that you identified yourself with externally and helped you to understand the importance of and how to identify with everything internally, as this is the source of everything and what connects you to everything and everyone.

You cannot identify with things that parish like possessions. A sign of when you are not in submission to your process is if your life feels choppy or if you feel like you are resisting. Submitting to your process feels like you are dancing effortlessly to music instead of being off beat, floating with the current of calm waters instead of trying to swim against the current, or demonstrating mastery of a form of martial arts instead of fighting with no cadence. A part of the process that you struggled with at first was releasing control of how and when things happen because it is scary, especially after operating with the pressure of "what's next?" your entire lifetime. The only way the universe can bring things together in a way you will never be able to fathom is through releasing control.

The plan that was laid out for you could not be successful without those who came before you, the environment that you were born in, and the people and places that you have and will encounter at different phases of your life. Your soul will never endanger your life, but it will always allow circumstances and people to bring lessons that mold you for the sake of fulfilling its purpose and giving you choice. Never lose or give away your sense of self, peace, or power. Trust your process by releasing control of the how and when, and live life in a way that you will not look back on with regret. Continue to love yourself unconditionally and know that everything that you need comes from within. Show people unconditional love and no judgment, and one person at a time, you can change the world.

Quote: "I am not everything I possess; I possess everything that I am." (*A Gift of Peace and Purpose: A Survivor's Journey*, p. 10)

Speak It: I am on a journey of peace and purpose, everything else is melting away.

Formula: Intention + Speak + Believe + Visualize + Emotion + Release + Action = What You Want

With all of the unconditional love from within,
The ME behind me

Dear Reader,

Thank you, from the bottom of my heart, for reading this book. My intention is to spark consciousness within you and format this book in a way that you can work through things at your own pace and with no judgment. In fact, I encourage you upfront to forgive yourself in advance, so that you can tell yourself the entire truth no matter how difficult it may be to embrace. In recognizing that everyone learns differently, this book provides many ways to get to the same result in which you can also complete the separate self-guided journal. If you are open to my suggestion, read the entire book at your own pace, and apply what makes sense to you.

I assure you that you can overcome anything through mindfulness, optimism, patience, persistence, self-love, and trust. It is my hope and prayer that at the end of this book, you will have or at least know how to get peace in your life, and you will be on, or at least recognize, the path to fulfilling your soul purpose in life. My goal is to capture not only that I survived what I thought was one of the worst things that could happen to me but also how my life experiences, people, and circumstances connected in a way that brought my entire life together so that you can do the same with yours without having to go through the headache of figuring it out like I did. This connectedness of life experiences positioned me to see how and why things were the way that they were. I hope and pray that you will feel encouraged to go on your own personal journey when you are ready and stay committed and optimistic. As you will see in this book, you can have peace and operate in your purpose.

What is at stake if you do not go on this journey is what is perceived as the negative side of life, repeating the same lesson, just with different people and places, being stuck in certain phases of your life, or never achieving your full potential. I feel the weight of life lifting off of you! I feel you taking your first breath of being alive! I feel your happiness and peace for you before it is already here! I see you in a place of peace and fulfillment while enjoying every moment of your life. I cannot wait to meet you and YOU.

With all of the unconditional love that I have,

Jeremy

Foresight

The year 2020 is the year that my cup ran over beyond what I could imagine. As I come to the end of 2019, I feel even more sure that I have gotten very close to doing everything that I was supposed to do in order to get where I am. Although I am not perfect, as I am human and I have made a lot of "mistakes" along the way, I am grateful for where I am. My journey will always continue with the difference from then and now of me being truly alive to know how to maneuver through a situation. It is almost like a dance that you learn, and over time you get better and better at it. My gift to the world is that of peace and purpose. They are gifts that can change the world for the better with no monetary value. It is a gift for the inside of every person, so that they can truly operate at their best within their purpose while being at peace. Everyone can reap that harvest of one thousand generations if they submit to the path and process needed to get to it.

What I Wish I Knew: Breaking the Cycle

In this moment of my life, I was pulling myself up and asking for a way out of a deep depression. I did not know that I was carrying generations of trauma on my back in addition to my own. My lens or perspective on life was broken, and I leaned toward trying to survive instead of thrive through honoring my purpose in life. I could not continue doing what previous generations had done because the outcome was the same every time; I had to break the cycle. Early on, had I known what I had been carrying and aware of the resources, such as therapy, I imagine I would be in a different place. I am grateful for the way life unfolded because peace and purpose became embedded into my DNA.

Having peace and purpose as a part of my DNA helped me to navigate life more easily. I had the space between circumstances, people, and myself to see the hidden lessons necessary for me to learn and apply. I also had the motivation to do the work, knowing the impact of my decisions were beyond my comprehension. Although my life did not immediately improve and was more "chaotic" than I imagined, it was truly divine perfection that made it all work.

Now I aim to make consistent and conscious choices aligned with peace and purpose. I understand that my life is mine to live as I please while knowing that my choices will always bring about circumstances and people that mold and shape me for my life's purpose. I now recognize my power comes from within through the connection of the source or that which created the human experience allowing me the power to design my life through the decisions I make with free will. With sacrifice of self and service to others through honoring purpose, life honors you in ways that some may only dream of. The journey of peace and purpose was challenging yet worth every step.

Love and Meditation: The Keys to Manifestation

Dear Me,

People often say that they wish they could go back in time and change things, and I say love yourself and meditate. I would go out on a limb and say that the journey of going through what we have was challenging but well worth the limitless possibilities because of practicing self-love and meditation. It is through self-love that you made peace with what has been done and cannot be changed. Love is something that we will continue to practice first with ourselves and then with others. It has genuinely been one of the ways that we have gotten to where we are now. By putting ourselves first, we have shown up for people in a more authentic, effective, and intentional way.

Through meditation, you reflected from a place of clarity to identify the root and impact of your behaviors that were not advantageous to our life. Meditation was supplemented with a mental health professional who helped you face our trauma and hurt head-on. This newfound understanding gives us the ability to make sounder decisions, knowing that there is an impact beyond what we can see. Loving yourself, meditating, and facing the hard truth helped us reveal who we indeed are. This daily practice of self-love and favorable conscious decisions is leading us to a life of fulfillment. Telling our story and painting a clear picture of how love and meditation is key to living a beautiful life will save people time and energy.

We must clearly convey the importance of ensuring that love and meditation is the air that people must breathe. I can see millions of people being positively impacted by this book as a result of those who read it allowing their higher sense of self to lead. These people who lead with their higher sense of self will go into the world making sound decisions in a way that convinces those who they interact with to do the same. I can feel the shift of energy that will take place as a result of people restoring themselves. It is such a beautiful thing to visualize people's lives changing because they routinely practice love of self and meditation.

With all of the unconditional love from within,

The ME behind me

Dear Reader,

I am writing this book to you as if I were writing it to myself when I was in a place of openness to receive the impossible. I know just through my little experience of life that it can be challenging to put yourself first and operate from a place of clarity. I hope you see how I began defining love of self and began making more intentional decisions for my well-being after dealing with my trauma and hurt head-on. I want you to embrace yourself in a way that you never even thought possible. Embrace the good, the bad, and the ugly of who you are because this is a part of what makes you unique and capable of great things. All of this is necessary to fulfill your purpose in life.

Everything you have encountered is for a reason and will never serve its positive intent until faced head-on. It is challenging to love yourself when you have never been taught to do so, have harbored a lot of negativity, and have internal noise distracting you. I want you to walk away with your own definition of love. I want to teach you how to operate from a place of clarity so that you can adequately deal with anything that comes your way. I want to help you manifest things that align with your purpose in life and the desires of your heart. I sincerely mean it when I say this: you are capable of all things that you put your mind to. Come along on this journey with me; I will hold your hand.

With all of the unconditional love that I have,

Jeremy

Dear Future Generation

If I were to set you up for success in the matters of meditation, I would tell you to focus on getting control of your mind as quickly as possible. Doing this helps you to make the best choices without all of the noise that comes with life. You have abilities beyond what the world tells you, and it is up to you to tap into them. This can only be done from a place of clarity. Without control of your mind, you may possibly end up in a cycle of life lessons that unfold as you make decisions from a place of survival. The goal is to identify your purpose in life as quickly as possible through looking at the deeper connections and meanings of the events that are happening in your life, apply the lesson learned, move forward, and do not stand still. Use your personal connection to the divine source, your higher sense of self, to bring circumstances and people into your life that will help you fulfill your purpose. You will receive everything you could ever desire on the other side of genuinely and with good intent chasing your purpose in life. Cherish each moment and enjoy the ride, your purpose will always provide.

What I Wish I Knew: Trust the Process

In this moment of my life, I was asking for a deeper relationship with myself and understanding why I went through what I went through. I did not know that I would have to begin defining things such as love. I thought it was obvious what love was, but there was a consistent disconnect between what some people said regarding love and what they did, including myself. I had to retreat inward, through meditation, to uproot the things that were causing me to not experience peace that was triggered by people's actions, including my own. By getting to the root of each issue that was showing up as something else in areas of my life, I could show up better and hold myself and other people accountable to what was truth rooted in good intention. I had to trust the process that things were unfolding in a way that was to my benefit regardless of my perception of the circumstance being good, bad, or ugly.

That inward experience on my quest for peace allowed me to also connect with God. A relationship with God, or the source, brings understanding and makes the impossible possible through very intentional decisions without control of the how and when. Had I known earlier that what also helped me attain peace was a necessary process of consistently going inward to allow my highest sense of self to lead, I imagine life would have been different. Despite this possibility, I am grateful.

Defining things like love allowed me to compare actions with words, making it easy to know what deserved my time and energy. The decision to only dedicate time and energy to what brought value to my life made space for things that needed to come into my life, such as circumstances and people, indirectly preparing me for my purpose. The more space that I had for myself, the more I realized my ability to design my life, through manifesting, in a way that made attaining purpose easy for me. This realization and the consistent practice of meditation was life changing because my personal power was now rooted in the core of who I was due to the things that were no longer serving me being released. I created the environment that made it easy for me to be in flow, calling things into my life with the intention of manifesting the life I deserved while honoring my purpose.

Lenses: Seeing the Unseen Spaces Between Us

Dear Me,

We are elevating higher and higher each round. It seems the higher we elevate spiritually, the more everything becomes magnified. The more we cleanse ourselves of things that clutter our life or pull us away from our purpose, the more intense our purpose, gifts, and talents become. Of course, with everything, there must be balance, the existence of equally extreme opposites. This is apparent when we experience these "swings" of low points as life unfolds.

We must give ourself grace, knowing that we are spiritual beings having a human experience. Thus, we are subject to stumbling sometimes. Having the self-awareness to view what we are going through holistically, as we stumble, is a gift many may never experience. I am proud of us for taking baby step after baby step to get to where we are, even if it took a while to get there. The important thing is that we make it to our destination, purpose fulfilled. But what happens when we "make it" and that which we have affirmed in private manifests? Have we done our due diligence in communicating and setting boundaries? Have we genuinely gotten to the root of all our issues? I feel the honest answer is no because this is an ongoing process.

When will the "right time" ever happen? The simple answer is, there is no right time; it simply happens when it happens. Just keep taking baby steps, it is not easy, but I feel that it will be well worth it to the core. Looking at the attitude of society pertaining to mental health, there seems to be a shift for the better. Celebrities are sharing their stories of childhood trauma, hurt, pain, and more making it "okay" to talk about these issues.

Hearing people such as Taraji P. Henson, Will Smith, and Adele coming forth and sharing their stories, Beyoncé making anthems about truly being alive despite all that you have been through, Issa Rae depicting real life in film, Oprah and Prince Harry making documentaries to share what people go through, and platforms such as *The Real*, *The Breakfast Club*, and *Red Table Talks* talking about mental health is needed, it is a collective effort for a greater good. The tides are shifting positively for those who have been suffering in the dark. This is the confirmation we need to keep pressing forward. We can help too. Even when it does not feel like we are equipped to handle what may come, everything will be alright. Through the course of nature and all that is the divine source, everything we need comes from within. The light at the end of the tunnel seems like it has been so close for so long. The difference is, when I close my eyes to visualize what I desire, I feel the warmth of the sun. We are almost there.

With all the unconditional love from within,
The ME behind me

Dear Reader,

Hold on. I know life has not been easy. I hope that this book will help you better navigate the path you are on to get through life a little easier. I am writing this book to help you disrupt the pattern of living in survival mode by offering my life as a reference point. Grinding everyday to survive makes it almost impossible to take time to truly process what is going on in our lives. Knowing that we are in control of our destinies, we owe it to ourselves to dig deep for life's lessons.

This is not an easy journey, but one well worth it. We all need tools, ideas, theories, or whatever works for us to get through this thing called life. Pointing out things that we all experience in life, I hope you can walk away changed for the better. You reading this book is a sign that positive change is possible and closer than you think. Hang in there. I will walk by your side.

With all of the unconditional love that I have,

Jeremy

Dear Future Generation

Lead with your highest sense of self by looking through your spiritual lens. This will never put you in a position to be hurt, but it will allow you to identify, learn, and apply life lessons more easily. Circumstances and people are used to bring these lessons to you as you go throughout this human experience. Lessons are necessary for you to be the best version of yourself so that you can honor your purpose in life. You must pull yourself into the present moment and make intentional choices that honor your purpose in life.

It is almost as if you are born into the world playing double Dutch. The people on each end of the rope represent systems as there are more than you. You represent humanity jumping in the middle, and the ropes spun are nature in its constant unfolding. Each rope represents circumstances and people meant to teach you lessons. For you to jump from between the ropes you must identify, learn, and apply the lesson. Look through your spiritual lens, and "SEE" everything around you to make intentional choices that will help you jump at the right time. Self-awareness is the key.

I learned of a Japanese term called *Ikigai*, which I understand to mean "A reason for being." It simply suggests your purpose lies at the heart of four principles: do something that you love, that the world needs, that you are great at, and that you can be paid for. With good intentions and aligning your actions toward your purpose, this concept is very genuine. Explore the world and try different things that do not harm you or put you in danger. Protect what is most sacred to you, but do not allow deep attachment to keep you from being open to new things.

In this limited life, we can never comprehend all things. What has been passed to you is only a fraction of what the world has to offer. The summation of what I do in my life can be viewed as the ceiling upon which you stand as a foundation for your life. Know that your purpose is the Sun, and you are the planets around it. Embrace that you are the planet, and use the power of your Sun to make life easier for those who need you. Everything that you need is within, release to receive while trusting the process and its unfolding. Everything will be alright.

What I Wish I Knew: Release to Receive

In this moment of my life, what I was asking for was the ability to connect the pieces of my life together. I did not realize that in order to do so, I must demonstrate an incomprehensible level of consistency in working on myself. There was and is so much work that an individual has to do in order to be granted access to a sense of knowing that is mind-blowing. You must have the inward space to operate at your highest potential by releasing to receive.

Making space for what is necessary to attain peace and purpose is more difficult than it seems. This may require breaking off relationships or things that are deeply rooted in your life. You cannot occupy one space with more than one thing; it will not last. My spiritual lens, or newly found perspective, allowed me to not only connect the pieces of life but also embrace that life is out of my control, beyond my decisions. With this understanding and knowing that I had authentic power, I had to hold myself accountable for my decisions.

I did not give my attention to things that were not in alignment with peace and purpose; although I am human. It became easy for me to release because I knew that my purpose was bigger and my personal resources were limited. I recognize that the decisions we make during this human experience are truly life or death, and I no longer wanted to walk around dead on the inside. Whatever it cost me to attain peace and purpose was a necessary sacrifice so that I could fulfill my reason for being and live the life that I deserved. Keeping in mind my decisions were the only thing in my control, I did my best as life unfolded. I had to ensure that my capacity was more than enough to take on what was coming next.

Well to the Soul:
Pouring from a Full Vessel

Dear Me,

I forgive you. Push, push, push. I forgive you. What is next? We must keep moving. I forgive you. We grew up quickly, as our childhood was a blur. We have distinct memories of love and laughter, yet we have a minimal recollection of childhood innocence. I give credit to you for surviving, but breathe deeply so we can live well.

We have the opportunity to ensure our capacity is sufficient as we pour into others. We can set an example of pouring from a full vessel with pure intent. We have the opportunity to help others protect their capacity to live a more present and intentional life. We are doing our due diligence to help people operate at their highest potential through self-awareness, which is something to be proud of. Remember to choose self first, avoiding the impulse to care for others' needs while abandoning your own. Let us give ourselves the grace we give others. This is the preparation season for what is to come.

With all the unconditional love from within,

The ME behind me

Dear Reader,

I am writing this book to you from a place of being tired and empty. In full transparency, this is a part of the journey we may be on together, and I may need you to hold my hand. For once, I am making an intentional effort to not be busy so that I can fill my vessel. I know that some of you may have tried or are in the process of doing this now. I think it is important to highlight what is at risk if we do not take this seriously.

What happens when we do not fill our vessels and continuously pour into others? How does our mind, body, and soul respond after years of putting ourselves second? Although this answer may be different for everyone, a possible answer that is common for us all is not living the life that we deserve. Let us give ourselves grace and the opportunity to fill our vessels. Let us establish consistent and intentional behaviors that allow us to be well and live well as we honor our soul's purpose. Hand in hand, we will press forward.

With all of the unconditional love that I have,

Jeremy

Dear Future Generation

Being of service to the world bears infinite fruit. It does not come easily, but I hope you see that it is possible through my actions. On the other side of chasing your purpose in life is everything you desire during this human experience. Up-front and temporary sacrifices of earthly desires yield eternal or long-term and sustainable success. I am not sure of the world you will inherit because of how quickly things change constantly. I can assure you that identifying your purpose as early as possible, combined with intentional and consistent efforts rooted in positivity to honor it with a full vessel, will allow you to soar higher than those who came before you, including myself.

We must help one another, being selfless by offering our purpose as a gift to the world. To add to that, love unconditionally without judgment, as we are all wonderfully and uniquely made. Aim to be and create the world you want for future generations, remembering that you are human, have limited capacity, and will one day pass the torch. As you align yourself with God or the source to co-create this life, remember to be patient, listen keenly, and see with your spiritual eyes. The human experience you inherit will require someone who knows and operates within their purpose, having the capacity to pour from a full vessel.

What I Wish I Knew: Chasing Purpose

In this moment of my life, I was asking for whatever was going to happen to happen. I did not know that it was happening, just not in a way that I could understand. Even though I had established a great relationship with myself, had understanding of why I went through certain things, knew how life connected, and knew that things were out of my control once I made my decision, it did not make it easy to maintain the right posture. I would argue that knowing that you are constantly doing the necessary steps could create a sense of anxiety in expectation of what is to come, especially when it has not manifested. I had to truly slow down and keep things off my plate so that I not only had the capacity but also used it intentionally to chase purpose.

We must respect that we have limited capacity in our human expression and must give ourselves the ability to restore, strengthen, increase, and protect that capacity. Without this, no amount of peace and motivation can sustain you long enough to fulfill your purpose. You cannot do what you cannot do. Listen to your body and protect it during this human experience.

It is imperative that we dedicate time to restore ourselves. As uncomfortable as it makes us to prioritize ourselves, disconnecting by going into our secret garden both figuratively and literally has to be a priority. Deciding not to ensure we have the right capacity leads to what we experience in our human expression as poor quality of life, disease, or unfortunately unanticipated death. Our purpose requires that we have inner peace that reflects on the outside and in our behaviors. Chasing purpose requires the capacity to run a marathon with no clear finish line.

Hidden Meadows: The Fulfilled Promise

Dear Me,

Let us go back to the unseen places. Dare to turnover every rock, lift up every carpet, and reexamine every shattered piece. We must do this knowing the impact it can have on our present life and future generations. Choosing a life of peace and purpose has had its challenging moments, but it has proven worth every step. From a place of peace, honoring our purpose in life is allowing us to create the life we deserve.

It is not about how and when it will happen, but about knowing that abundance is our portion with the positive intent we have sown in every seed we have planted. A life of abundance can be easily taken away and it is up to us to ensure we have done our part to be ready to handle it. Maximizing this human experience is an opportunity that many may feel is too heavy a lift, but we can lighten the load. Let us continue our individual journey of peace and purpose, knowing that abundance is on the other side. Not for materialistic gain, but for fulfillment of our purpose, leaving the world a better place for the generations to come.

With all the unconditional love from within,

The ME behind me

Dear Reader,

I am still on my journey of peace and purpose, and I am making progress. A part of what keeps me motivated is knowing the impact the decisions in my life will have on future generations. In writing this book, I hope that you too realize what is at stake when we do not live a life of peace and purpose. It is fair to live your life how you decide to live it; after all it is your life. I encourage you to look deep to examine the underlying reason for any decisions you make during this human experience by asking yourself *why am I making this decision?*

Even the smallest decision we think is nothing can suggest a tie to behaviors from conditioning, trauma, or even prior generations. This small glimmer of awareness is just enough to ensure your behaviors, although focused on self, have positive intent given the indirect influence they may have on others. At a minimum, choose to live a life of peace so that those around you can do the same. If you should be so daring, adding purpose can positively shift your life in ways unimaginable. Abundance is within each opportunity, if we dare to embark on the journey of peace and purpose.

With all of the unconditional love that I have,

Jeremy

Dear Future Generation

It is my hope that you can see and appreciate the work that has been done to ensure you have a life of abundance. It is now your turn to take what has been given to you to quickly find inner peace and your purpose in life, so that you can do the same for future generations. I know, even before you reach adulthood or before you are even born, that life will not be the same for me as it is for you. Know that the efforts to provide you with this compass to navigate life is rooted in unconditional love.

Find inner peace to operate from a place of clarity and love. Identify and honor your purpose in life, so that you can be of service to people, making their life a little easier. Trust the process, knowing that everything you need is being pulled from within as you encounter circumstances and people. Be comfortable with releasing to receive so that you carry what is relevant to your inner peace and purpose. Chase purpose so that everything can follow, leading you to a life of abundance and fulfillment.

What I Wish I Knew: Abundance

In this moment of my life, I was asking for consistency in my actions. I knew that everything would unfold at the right time and in the right way. I was at peace knowing that I was doing my part by making conscious and consistent choices to honor my purpose. Regardless of how it looked on the outside, I knew that I was planting the necessary seeds that would eventually turn into an endless abundance harvest. There was nothing left for me to do but remain consistent in my actions and posture, remain in flow.

I realized that my extreme desire to attain something tangible was sending out mixed messages, and that I had to stop. Gratefulness became my every thought. Peace kept me clear. Purpose kept me going. When signs would affirm that harvest season was getting close, I was encouraged to remain consistent.

As often as I heard it, the saying about consistency over perfection never hit home until this journey. I was far from perfect on this journey of peace and purpose, yet my consistency pulled me closer every step of the way. The opportunities that began to happen were like portals that moved me closer to the finish line. It was important to ensure that I remained in alignment and flow by allowing my highest sense of self to make purpose-oriented decisions. I now realize that even with all the pieces in order, I still had to jump head-first into relevant opportunities that made honoring my purpose possible despite how uncomfortable it was. I knew my intention was pure, so my purpose took precedent over my comfortability. My comfort zone had to disappear if I wanted to leave the world better than it was when I got here.

Now, I maintain the posture that suggest *it is already done.* I am just waiting for it to tangibly manifest. When and how are irrelevant while doing the best I can with what I have remains critical. There is no need to worry or be anxious as this creates a disconnect between what we desire our reality to be when we have done our part. Inner peace and fulfillment of our purpose in life is the goal. Abundance remains the indirect winning of a life of peace and purpose.

Dear Future Generation

Please receive these letters as a token of my love and desire to ensure you live the life you deserve. What you do with your life is up to you. By the time that you are in a space to process this entire body of work, I hope that you realize you have only experienced the abundance life has to offer due to the harvest being reaped from the seeds sown before you. I hope that you then start your own journey of peace and purpose to begin sowing seeds with positive intent that will continue the harvest that you are enjoying as future generations will follow you. Remember that you are simply a vessel with limited capacity being used to fulfill a unique purpose during this human experience. With inner peace, you can navigate life more easily, seeing the deeper meaning of life intended to ready you for your purpose. Love and meditation will help.

May this body of work be the compass you use when you need direction. Each decision you make will create a ripple that goes beyond what your mind can fathom. The conscious and consistent choice to align each decision you make with peace and purpose will yield an abundant life as you may now be able to see and comprehend. Know that regardless of your choice to pursue a life of peace and purpose or not, extreme efforts were made to help you have that choice and live the life you deserve out of unconditional love. Despite my inevitable absence in this human expression, from a spiritual plane, I am always there waiting to love and guide you.

With love that surpasses time, space, and energy,

Jeremy

From my Mom with Love

My future generation, I am so happy that I have an opportunity to write you this letter. There is nothing new under the sun. My hope for you is that you are able to experience life to the fullest. Do not allow the trials that may come to completely derail your dreams. It does not matter what life throws at you; it matters how you handle it.

Within each circumstance is a lesson to be learned that will prepare you for the next step. However, if you do not learn the lesson, you will repeat the circumstances until you understand the deeper meaning. They say that insanity is making the same decisions but expecting different results. Make decisions with your end goal in mind. To the best of my ability, I will guide you with what I know as my love for you is unconditional.

I cannot tell you how to live your life, but I will offer advice that has kept me standing. Do not focus on what people will say about you. Do not allow their thoughts about you to control you. Stay focused on your goals while being true to yourself. You are the author of your success, claim it and own it. Stay humble as life will always test your character.

Love You As You Are,

Mama V

Conclusion

I encourage you to make each decision knowing that someone will inherit the fruits of your labor. It is my hope that you realize the potential that you have to live a life of abundance through a life of inner peace and honoring your life's purpose. Regardless of your choice, accept that what you put into this human experience is what you will reap. Choose something that you can reap forever. Choose something that you would want to inherit.

What will you make of the time that you have during this human experience? Will you use it to continue all cycles that you may have been born into? Will you put forth the effort to break the cycles that do not serve value in pursuit of a life of peace and purpose? What do you want to be true when you are at the end of this human experience? Remember, there is never a wrong time to start the journey to a life of peace and purpose.